The RHYTHM of HEART

SONU GURU

Rhythms of Heart

Copyright © 2025 Sonu Guru

All rights reserved. No part of this book may be reproduced, stored in a retrieval system, or transmitted in any form or by any means, electronic, mechanical, photocopying, recording, or otherwise, without the prior written permission of the author.

This book is sold as is, without any warranties, express or implied. The author and publisher are not responsible for any problems that may arise from using this book. If you have a problem with the book, your only option is to return it for a refund. The author agrees to protect the publisher from any legal issues that may arise from the book's content. Any legal disputes about this book will be handled according to the laws of the constitution of India

Publisher: Inkscribe Media Pvt. Ltd

ISBN Number: 978-1-966421-37-5

I want to dedicate this book to the silence and muse of life.

Contents

Foreword	7
Preface	9
Acknowledgments	11
Splendid Sky	13
I Wish I Could Write a Poem	16
Nature	18
Journey Ahead	20
Purpose of Life	22
Meadows	24
Influencer	26
Sun	28
Wind	30
In the Morning Light	32
Teacher	34
School Life	36
Bird with Wings	38
Leaf	40
Kids	42
Art	44

Foreword

Poetry is a heartfelt journey of words expressed in most subtle way. In this collection Sonu Guru, expresses intricate balance between nature and emotions. Weaving the human experiences into poetic environment.

'Rhythms of Heart', a collection of short poetry is a debut poetry book published by Sonu Guru. Her work portrays nature in its most delicate form that can sensitise human soul and can discover peace amidst chaos. Her work discovers meaning of existence and beyond. To navigate life through silence and muse. Her collection is also dedicated to various phases of life and inspirations.

Preface

My poetry depicts nature and the intricate balance between nature and our emotions and the fact that we are one with nature and the trials and tribulations of a pure sensitive soul that tries to find answers in nature and its various facets. To navigate life in the solace that nature provides.

Acknowledgments

I am deeply grateful to everyone who has made this possible for me. Turning my passion for writing into a book.

To my family who have always tried to understand and encourage my poetic side.

To my little daughter for her beautiful drawings. To my silent thoughts and ideas.

To countless experiences and inspirations from various phases of life.

Splendid Sky

Sky, you are high up there,
      Where do you find solace?
Is it in the midst of ripples of flowing river,
      Or in the rustling of ocean waves,
You're lost in the mayhem of noise.

What is your colour?
      Is it the flash of sunshine,
Or the beaming white,
      Is it the depth of blue haze,
Or snowy grays,

Where do you reside?
      In the shivering silence of flowing wind,
Or in the picturesque vastness of valley,
      You're lost in the noise of thunderstorms,
Or in the delicate drops of pouring rainfall,

When do you laugh?
        In the innocence of a lamb,
Or in the hustles of human existence,

You fill us with wonder & splendor,
        You are splendid,
You are sky.

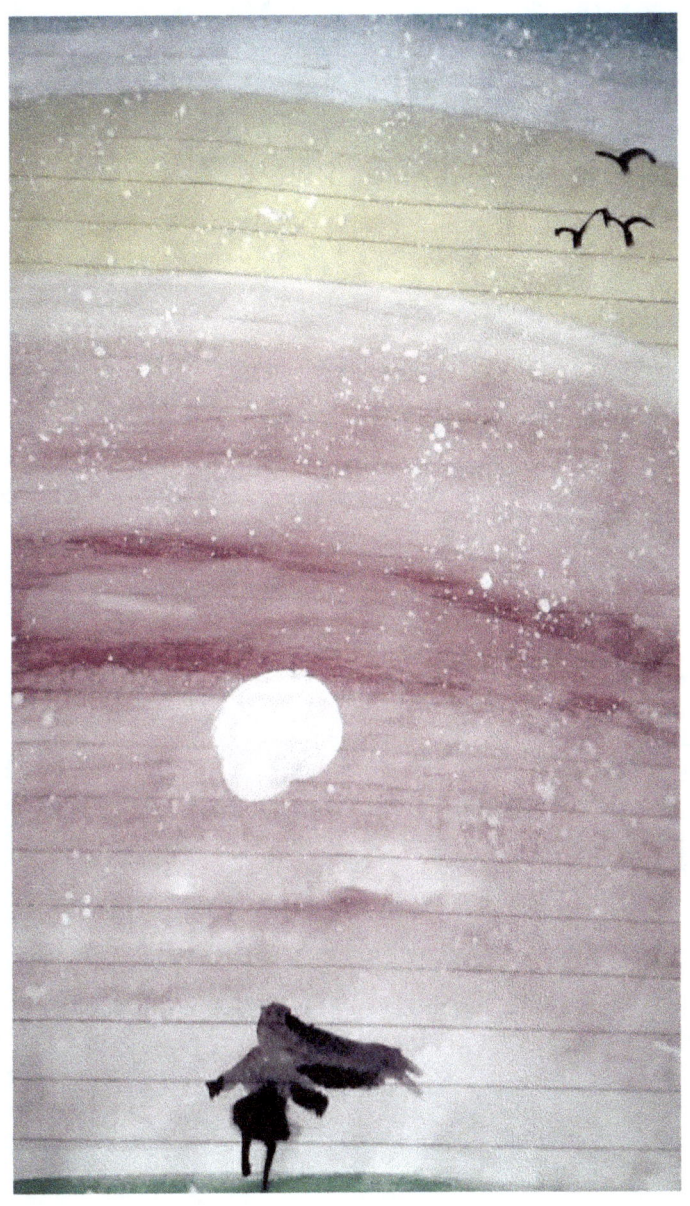

I Wish I Could Write a Poem

I wish I could write a poem,
      To search the rising sunshine,
To dwell the time elapsed,
      To search that is lost,

To meet my present,
      To see the unending sky,
To sit under the shady tree,
      To ask the sunlight to come back tomorrow,

After meeting that sweet dawn,
      I return to meet my puzzled heart,
To call, search and adorn tomorrow,
      I wish I could write a poem.

Nature

Nature you stand, you fall,
      You surprise, you fight
Keep silence,
      Show vigour in times,
Lost in the triumph of civilization,
      Unending potrayal of desire and despair,
Sometimes gloomy,
      Sometimes bright,
Nurturing the soothing sight.

Journey Ahead

Leaving the whimperings behind,
      forging for the challenges ahead,
that's life, that's untold story of life.

Listening to the hymns of hopes,
      Standing under the beaming sunlight
Searching for the shadyside
      Putting together all the strength
Paving for the unknown trials
      Reaching for the unseen heights

God has given us all in abundance
      Praising his creation is our reverence
Peace and solitude is all we wish for
      But do we get it in all?

With hope as our compass,
      we'll find our way,
Chasing the dawn of a brighter day.

Purpose of Life

What is the purpose of life?
    Is it exploring the world
Or journey within,
    Finding peace or facing challenge,
How to search for an aim,
    amidst the chaos.
When life brings numerous questions unanswered.
    It's an examination without preparation

Getting to know yourself is an expectation.
    Explore the world,
discover the truth,
    and knowing yourself.
is the journey to be pursued.

Meadows

Meadows you travel
      Beneath the sky.
Besides the river.
      Following the clouds.
Exploring the mysteries.
      Embracing the wind.
Glaring at the Sun.
      Dozing near the tree.
To revive.
      To nurture.
To quench your quest.

Influencer

Influencer
      A celebrity in present era,
I mean my words,
      I speak my heart,
I get million views,
      I sing for art,
I dance like noone's watching,
      I am the performer,
I am the star,
      I don't need script,
I don't need crew,
      I take break cause I feel that way.
I influence cause I have it in me.
      My subscribers show up for me.
I get love, I may get hate,
      But I come up with new ideas everyday,
I like to create for the viewer's sake.
      I am a free spirited creator,
I am influencer.

Sun

You are the radiance of the sky.
      Amidst the dark foggy clouds.
Giving hope and faith.
      To the puzzled souls.
To the world of melancholy.

Wind

Oh winds! give me your pace to fly,
      Cause you fly up in the sky,
In the midst of mystery & surprise,
      Find solace in the shadow of silence.

In the Morning Light

In the morning light,
    Sun rise up in the sky,
Waking million people,
    Showing up for their dreams,
Nurturing the flora and fauna,
    Giving warmth to the God's creation,
Giving hope to the new beginnings,
    Getting lost in the innocence of a child,
Praising the beauty of nature's delight.
    Witnessing the hustle of human spirit,
Glowing dews of moist grass,
    Steady breeze freshens up the pass,
In the morning light.

Teacher

A kind soul,
>A guiding light in the dark,

A ray of hope amidst chaos,
>A mentor in a confusion,

A facilitator for the young mind,
>A future builder,

A trailblazer for a generation,
>Shaping millions dreams to reality,

Paving way with all the humility,
>Giving meaning to exploration,

Adding life to ignorance.

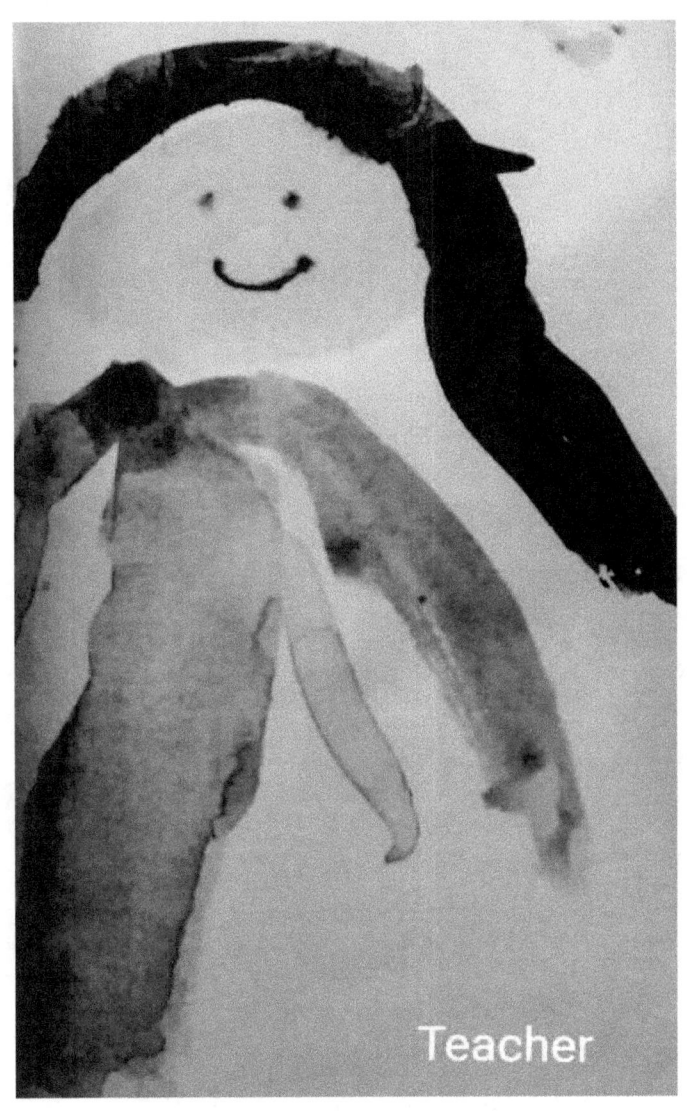

School Life

Studies between the ring bells,
> Hush - hush between the teacher's stare,

Walking across the corridors,
> Taking each step towards the aim,

School life is memory of a lifetime.

Feeling lazy during the morning assembly,
> to running like a freebie in a playground,

Sharing lunch with your friends,
> to forgetting assignments at home,

School life is a memorable time.

Preparing for functions nonstop,
> to taking breaks in canteen,

Feeling nervous for exams,
> to getting marks in result day,

Weaving numerous dreams in mind,
> School life is an unforgettable time.

Bird with Wings

To spread peace and love,
      I see kids playing,
I see mothers nurturing,
      I see people working,
I fly to heal,
      I fly to bless,
I dread tears,
      I dread pain,
I doubt hate,
      and discard bane,
I pray for the world,
      Wish it loves, laughs
and sustain.

Leaf

Leaf you are
      So petite, So fragile,
So soft, So delicate,
      Do you reside in the frisk of tree,
Or seek pleasure in the flowing wind,
      Where do you fall ?
In the midst of surprise,
      Or in the depth of reality.

Kids

The symbol of innocence,
    The picture of sunshine,
The bundle of cheer,
    The portrayal of mischief.
The laughter that dances,
    The whispers of dreams.

Art

Draw to melt,
        Sing to resonate,
Dance to fly,
        Art flows through the shadows of sentiments.
Art defines the magic that resides.

Breaking the boundaries of silent walls,
        Reaching the heart that hears its soul.
Making its way through tests and turmoil.
        Shines amidst the shady toil.

I extend my deepest gratitude for the completion of the book.